I0162603

Advance Praise

As a family therapist, I appreciate the opportunity to be able to have Ms. Miller's book to add to my arsenal of support for my clients.

Working with women and men who are transitioning into a new phase of life, sometimes it is beneficial to be able to share a book with them that can contribute to their journey.

One of the difficulties in doing this is being aware of the client's level of understanding, and where they are in their journey.

The book needs to fit into so many niches, such as:

*Is it entertaining enough to keep their attention?

*Will the client be able to identify with what the author is saying?

*Does the book have useful information?

I believe Ms. Miller's book fulfills all those requirements nicely. Women (and men) will be able to feel part of Ms. Miller's journey and know that her experience can apply to them.

Ms. Miller is very open and real in sharing her experiences in a way that isn't off-putting to either sex.

~ Dr. Debra J. Lee-Moreno, LMFT

Advance Praise Cont.

Miller's stories share the triumphs and lessons learned from dating through her 20s, 30s and beyond, giving raw advice, gentle encouragement, real-life examples and in-your-face facts about dating to find the perfect match. Though some are lucky (or settle) to have someone earlier in life, Miller clearly demonstrates that finding the right match takes work—from both sides. It would do anyone struggling to find the right person a bit of good to spend some time reading this book to see how one person keeps perspective and her focus as she winds her way through this frustrating, oft-dead-ended dating conundrum.

~Joe Wessels, journalist, columnist, talk radio show host, blogger.

Single ~ YES!
Lonely ~ NO!

C. Lee Miller

Copyright © 2016 C. Lee Miller

All rights reserved.

ISBN:0692336982
ISBN-13:9780692336984

DEDICATION

To my family and my family of friends.

Table of Contents

Appreciation and Acknowledgments

Thank you to my "sisters" and my "brothers"... I've missed a few birthday parties, a few holiday dinners and many happy hours because I've been focused on my writing. Thank you for your encouragement and support.

M.L. – I thought you were crazy when you said I should write this book; I'm so thankful I listened to you!

Sean Donegan and Mick Coyle, my computer guys, you were both always so helpful with my little glitches - thank you!

A big THANK YOU to my teacher and writing coach, Judith Cassis, who provided me with inspiration and guidance.

Another big THANK YOU goes out to my fellow classmates ... the best audience I could ever ask for to critique my work. They've sat through numerous classes listening to my thoughts without judgment; they've also inspired and guided me through this wonderful, yet challenging journey.

A shout-out to my editor, Natalie Buhl. WOW! I should have paid more attention in Mrs. Stidger's English class. Who knew I could dangle so many participles? You had your work cut out for you! Great job! Thank you!

Sarah Szymanski, my proofreader - thank you for taking time out of your busy schedule to read and re-read this book!

To Ethel Lee Miller, author of *Seedlings, Stories of Relationships* - thank you for giving this book the professional polish it needed. You made it comfortable for me to take the next step.

The cover of this book was drawn by my cousin, Sharon Ludwig. She is not a biological cousin; she is someone I adopted in my heart.

After one of her visits to Southern California, as a thank you for being her hostess, she drew this picture of me. Can you imagine my emotions as I opened the package? As soon as I saw it, I knew it would become the cover of my book!

The butterfly tattoo on my shoulder (featured in the drawing) has a story, as do many people's choices of ink. My first tattoo needed to go; it was a tribute to the childhood I'd outgrown. I went to see an artist and explained the need to cover up my past and move forward … into my future. I decided on a butterfly design. Once the work was completed and I saw it in all it's glory, I was so happy that I called my mom to share my news. She asked repeatedly about my choice of a butterfly, but I didn't have an answer for her; it was just something I picked because it was pretty.

At that time in my mom's life she was reading a therapeutic self-help book. When she got to the last section of her book, there it was, on the page: a big beautiful butterfly! That chapter was titled "Freedom." Once she made the connection between the chapter called "Freedom" and my new butterfly tattoo, she called me. It spoke to both of us in a personal way. We allowed ourselves to be free of our pasts and move forward in our lives with no regrets. You can't cover up your past as I did with a tattoo, but you can change a few things to brighten your future.

IT'S NOT THEM ... IT'S ME

It's not them ... It's me

So open, so free ... I don't care is what I say ... maybe I want it the other way.

Being independent, being strong ... how can that be wrong?

Living my life the way I want ... is there something I'm missing?

Someone I should be kissing?

Who is that one? Who could that be? The one that is supposed to be with me ...

~C. Lee Miller, written after a significant break-up

Introduction

I am single. I can hardly believe that I've managed to stay single into my 40s! I must be on the catch-n-release program when it comes to dating. I have had many long-term relationships and have been asked to marry, but have chosen to remain single due to my intense fear of regret and, subconsciously, a lack of trust. My first "more-than-a-summer-fling" boyfriend at the ripe 'ole age of 21 was married, but I didn't know that at the time. He lived in a different state, and his business brought him to my hometown often. Once I found out his secret, our relationship ended. My second boyfriend joined the military, and due to the distance that one ended. So began my circle of dating.

A few of my past boyfriends wanted to be married and since I was not interested, they moved on to find someone they could marry. One of my exes even invited me to his wedding! I chose to only attend the reception – I felt that was a compromise. He and I still e-mail every so often, just to stay in touch. I have actually stayed in contact with several of the guys I've dated in the past. We now have a different type of relationship; we are friends.

Foreword

Depending on where and when you grew up, dating rituals differ. I've been told through stories from older friends and family that dating rituals in the past would consist of groups of girlfriends who would go out to a local dance hall or an open wedding reception to mingle with the hopes of meeting a guy and exchanging phone numbers for a future, more formal date, such as dinner and a movie.

Dating today follows different trends—there's speed dating, sport dating and on-line dating. Today there's an aura of freedom to dating, less for commitment ... dating for companionship versus finding a life partner. The pressure for me to find a husband has lightened significantly. During my 20s and 30s, many of my girlfriends' mothers or grandmothers would often ask me, "When are you going to find a man?" I would reply, "Oh believe me – I've found plenty!"

As dating trends have changed, committed relationships have also changed ... they've progressed. Today we hear more about same sex marriage, as well as commitment ceremonies between two people who choose only to be "married" in their hearts and don't feel the need for a legal document. This type of relationship is a beneficial way to spend your later years in life when each of you have already raised a family, earned your retirement funds, and support your own health care program.

There are many types of relationships - traditional and untraditional - which I share with you in this book.

Red Rover, Red Rover ... Think about your happiness over and over.

SUCCESSFULLY SINGLE

Awhile back my dad came to visit me in Southern California. As he looked around my condo, he began to weep. I asked him, "Dad, what's wrong?" He replied, "Nothing, absolutely nothing is wrong."

He was overwhelmed with pride.

Dad said, "I always had your mom to help me and your sister has her husband, but you ... you do this all by yourself."

To be recognized by my father as an independent, strong-willed, hardworking, happy woman made me proud of myself. I'll never forget that moment.

Single - YES! Lonely - NO!

Sometimes my independence gets in the way of my long-term relationships. I like to know and show that I can do what I want, when I want, and with whom I want.

Here's an example: My high school girlfriend asked me to go out of town with her to celebrate her birthday. She had also invited an ex-boyfriend of mine who is still in my life as a very close friend. I said yes to her invite right away because I knew I'd love to go and help her celebrate, as would our mutual close friend.

I was in an on-and-off again relationship for a couple of years; it just so happened that at the time of the invitation, our relationship switch was in the "on" position, so technically, he was my boyfriend. He strongly disagreed with the idea of me going out of town with this group of friends, one being a part of my ex-files. None of us going on the trip wanted him to go because of our on and off situation; we couldn't fully trust it to be a "birthday celebration" vacation since he was not comfortable with me spending time with an ex-boyfriend. I had a decision to make, and I chose not to let my "on-and-off again guy" make this decision for me. I needed to protect my fear of regrets. The situation may have been different had I been in a strong, secure relationship – but as it was, it was flimsy. I felt I didn't need permission to live my life; this was something I wanted to do, so I went and had a great time with my friends. I felt I made the right decision for myself; I felt confident and strong-willed; I felt independent and happy.

A few months after my return, we broke up for the last time. I became single again … and that was okay with me!

IT'S THE LITTLE THINGS IN LIFE

Contrary to popular belief, not all women pay a lot of attention to their "internal biological clock." Some women, including myself, choose not to have children but that doesn't mean we don't enjoy spending time with the little ones. There was a period in my young adult life when I chose to date guys who had a child or children. Dating someone with kids allowed me to spend my "kid energy" without having to be a parent 24 hours a day, 7 days a week.

Dating someone who had joint custody was a wonderful situation. There was alone time with my guy, and there was time to spend with his kids. The activities

5

with the children were planned, executed, and completed in a timely manner.

Dating someone with kids is a different kind of relationship. You could very well end up liking the kids more than their dad. Or, you could, as I've experienced, like the guy more than the kids. Then what do you do? It's a big decision–but it's yours to make.

If I happen to be single and want to go catch the latest Disney movie, I might … borrow my friends children.

Borrowing your friends' children is different than babysitting because it's your time frame, your idea.

Babysitting is when the parent or parents call you for assistance when they need you.

For many years, having a single-mother friend in my life has benefited me, my friend, and her children. I am her kids guardian for a few hours.

I benefit from knowing that I am helping a friend and helping mold society's future. She benefits by getting some time to herself to run errands, clean the house, relax or go out with her friends. The children benefit by knowing that they have another adult in their lives who loves them

6

unconditionally and truly wants to be in their company. I am someone they can turn to if their parent is not the one they choose to communicate with about specific topics. I am a liaison. A conduit. A go-between. Someone they can trust. If the children confide in me and I feel my friend needs to know, then I can share that information as a third party.

Maybe you're the fun neighbor that likes to bake. It would be sweet to invite the child over to help out and then send them home with some treats and a story to share about their experience. Do you remember an adult who was there for you as a child? Maybe it was your favorite aunt you always looked forward to seeing and shared special moments together. Keep in mind that borrowing children could have a limited time frame. As they grow older, they may not want to spend time with you; they may choose to spend more time with their friends. You could feel let down emotionally. Not to worry, there are plenty of young people out there—find them. Don't know where to find them? Volunteer for a children's charity.

Single - YES! Lonely - NO!

In the past, I've volunteered for a foster children's charity, a local charity that hosts two large festivals a year geared towards the children. They also host fund-raisers; I was sure to be on their mailing list.

Volunteering for this type of charity gave me satisfaction knowing I was there for the children and their host families. Many children are placed in foster care through no fault of their own. These children need inspiration and guidance, and they are typically open to sharing time with strangers who meet their needs for the day. You can sign up to be a volunteer, as I did, which would include, but not be limited to: setting up and serving the food, organizing the give-away items, supervising the younger volunteers and being available for situations that arise unexpectedly. OR … you can sign up to be a mentor for the day and if you feel you made a solid connection with your assigned child, then you could become their mentor long-term. As a mentor to these kids, there is a huge responsibility to be there for them and not let them down, for they've already experienced the feeling of being let down in their short lifetimes. A mentor can provide encouragement and stability.

Making memories … Smile and say cheese!

ALL ABOARD THE MIGHTY SHIPS

From Friendships to Relationships

As stated previously, there are so many different types of relationships. It's been rewarding to me to have opposite sex "friends without benefits" in my life. I refer to them as "without benefits" because there is no way, shape, form or fashion that these friends will ever become my significant other. With this team of friends there are no barriers, no filters and only superficial expectations. I can be my true self – these friends are my support team.

I have relationships with my neighbors. I have a neighbor who I invite over for coffee or sometimes a cocktail. Some neighbors I give the bare minimum - like an

11

annoying neighbor who just gets the "Hi – I'm picking up my mail" wave.

There are co-worker relationships ... some I only see during business hours or after work functions. I have a close relationship with them but don't make plans with them unless it is work related. I have a strong business relationship with some folks in other departments ... I know, if necessary, they will stay late and get my package shipped out. Then there are those co-workers who become friends outside of the workplace - ones you'd enjoy hanging out with on the weekends or grabbing a cold one with after work.

You may have a relationship with a waiter or waitress at your favorite restaurant – someone who is happy to see you, where the banter goes further than, "How are you today?" Once you start chatting about your interests, you could find that you both enjoy hiking or camping. This could lead to a new experience, a new location ... meeting more new people. If you choose to make plans for an outdoor adventure - you can be in charge of the picnic lunch.

I have a wonderful relationship with my hair stylist. Not only do we get to catch-up while I'm getting my hair cut but, by talking, we discovered that we have so much in common that we are now comfortable enough to plan adventures and are open to spending time together outside the salon.

Having a friend who enjoys sports, or if you know someone who plays a sport on the weekends, offer to go cheer them on. Going out to their event could lead to hanging out afterwards to talk about the game. It could lead to joining each other for a local sporting event or watching one on TV. Pick a player to root for and make a silly bet.

Do you enjoy traveling? Certainly there is someone in your circle of friends with whom you can plan a weekend get-away. Start with a small weekend outing; not everyone can get along for an extended period of time. Once you get comfortable, you can begin to plan a longer, more intense trip.

Single - YES! Lonely - NO!

These are rewarding types of friendships – get on board!

Once I begin to date someone who I choose to include in my life as a steady, romantic partner, I explain that I have many friends both male and female and I am not willing to give up my special friendships. There has been some jealousy involved, but I convey there should be no threat.

A few of my past boyfriends and I started as just friends; they already knew me as the fun-loving soul who enjoyed quality and quantity time with long term friends outside the relationship. I explained that spending time with others can actually enhance our intimate relationship. That being glued to the hip of each other would cheat us out of enjoying the diversity life has to offer.

The right partner should be able accept you and all your friends. If your new mate cannot understand that you have a variety of friends, make him walk the plank.

Is her real name Lucky?

NICKNAMES

If you are outgoing and like to talk to just about anyone, you may start to accumulate new acquaintances in your life. My friends and I tend to give nicknames to these new people we meet; it's easier to keep track of them this way.

Nicknames for people you have in your circle of friends can extend to friends who don't know each other. My girlfriend, Lightning, doesn't know my girlfriend Enchilada, but when I talk to them about the other person, they recollect stories of the past just by reference to their nicknames.

How do you get a nickname ... or give one for that matter? Nicknames could describe your occupation, like in the following example: I met two guys through a mutual friend; they were both named Jay. One was a plumber, so we called him Plumber Jay. The other one we called Gay Jay, even though he is not gay; he just seemed happy all the time. Another occupational nickname was given to a guy I met who worked in a smoke shop; we nicknamed him Chong. I told him that my friends and I called him Chong, and he was excited about the nickname we gave him; he liked it. He was not in my life long enough to be called by his real name; no one even remembers what his real name is—so we still refer to him as Chong.

You can also get a nickname during an activity, such as a night of bowling. One I received was Butta' because Buttercup Banana Buns did not fit on the bowling score screen.

Another way to give a nickname could be by actions, such as, a girlfriend of mine nicknamed one of her new interests Marshmallow Man. She said his penis was so limp while trying to have intercourse that it was like stuffing a marshmallow into a keyhole. The poor guy was referred to as Marshmallow Man throughout the duration of their relationship. He didn't last very long. (No pun intended) She soon moved on to a guy she nicknamed Freeway because she met him while driving on the freeway, and that relationship lasted over two years!

Here's an example of how nicknames can be beneficial: another girlfriend of mine has a son named Bryan. Coincidently, she started seeing a guy named Brian. When I received an e-mail or text from her, I knew which one she was talking about because of the difference in the spelling; however, if we were having a phone conversation, it could go either way ... "Bryan and I went to the movies." The whole time I was thinking BRIAN! I told her, "Enough already. Give the guy you are seeing a nickname so I can keep the stories straight from the beginning." We started referring to him by his initials. Whew!

I've often wondered if any of my past boyfriends had a nickname for me while dating. Since I tend to talk louder than the average bear, I can assume at one point or another one of them has referred to me as Loud Girl. I can imagine them saying, "Loud Girl and I went to dinner last night." My name is not important to his friends, associates, or co-workers at this point because we've just met.

This works perfectly when you meet a guy and want to tell your friends about him, but they don't really need to invest a lot of energy into remembering another Matt or Jim. Unless you're my friend of many years with the nickname Glendale Jim. My long-time friend, Jim, used to live in the city of Glendale, but now has moved to Monrovia. We still call him Glendale Jim since Monrovia Jim just doesn't fit.

In the dating world, once you start calling your new man by his real name, it's a sign that the relationship is growing. Your friends and family will recognize the transition by using his first name, too.

Like the X's and O's of Tic-Tac-Toe ... They go together.

CHEMISTRY

Ahhh ... Chemistry between two people, what a wonderful feeling!

According to Webster's dictionary, chemistry is the study of substances and their production or conversion. That definition doesn't seem to encompass the chemistry feeling between potential partners. So, how do you find the type of chemistry felt between two people?

It can be found by engaging with others on a daily basis. We don't meet all the people we surround ourselves with, whether at the grocery store or the gym, but we are drawn to certain ones that makes our heart beat a little faster or give us the feeling of butterflies in our stomach—a feeling that we should actually meet that certain one, keeping a close eye on him to see if he looks in your direction and possibly nods or smiles.

How do you get beyond casual glances and actually meet this person?

If you feel you are ready to start up a conversation, you can use the age-old question, "Do you come here often?" It's a casual question but one which will give you the answer to what you want to know. If he is a local, then there's something to build on, and if he is just passing through your neighborhood, his answer may open the conversation to talk about where he does live or the area in which he works. You'll never know until you try! Maybe I'm jumping ahead; you just laid eyes on him … but it's advice to consider if you are prepared for that glance to turn into romance. Let's see where this is going …

Are Men and Women Truly Opposites?

Some studies indicate that males and females from childhood to adulthood are more alike than different on most psychological variables. Both men and women like to be appreciated and complimented. Most people, gender aside, know right from wrong. These are variables that typically do not fluctuate with age.

But what about the saying, "Opposites attract"? This may refer to the bookworm who is attracted to the athlete or the snow bunny attracted to the surfer dude.

As other studies show, men and women are different, not necessarily opposites. I like this idea. Dating someone who sees the world differently than you do can bring balance into your lives. You can introduce him to something you enjoy and then join him in an activity he enjoys. There's excitement in sharing some of your favorite activities and places with him and in letting him show you new things. I have dated the jock, the musician and the car mechanic. I had to respect our differences as I haven't played a team sport since middle school, all who know me know I can't carry a tune, nor have I ever fixed my own car. The jock practiced, which left me time for myself, the musician slept in and stayed up late (whereas I have a 9-5 job) and the mechanic enjoyed his alone time facing under the hood of a car. Did I attend their games? Did I go to the weekend gigs? Did I attend many a car show? I did because these activities were important to build on the chemistry-base we'd already established. Communicate and compromise so there's a respectful outcome.

A tisket a tasket. What should I put in my basket?

WANTS AND NEEDS

When I was a little girl, my parents were quick to teach me the difference between wants and needs. As a child, I wanted to run around and play all day. I needed supervision and guidance. As a teenager, I wanted Guess jeans. (Yes, I grew up in the 80s.) I needed pants. As an adult, I can better determine my wants and needs and turn them into reality; I seek unconditional love from the people who are secured in my life.

What are you looking for in a partner? Is it someone who is tall, dark and handsome? Those are some proverbial wants.

Single – YES! Lonely – NO!

In reality, your needs may include similar personality traits, educational background, level of physical fitness, life goals, and possibly the same religious beliefs. Levels of compatibility would include things such as: you're both vegetarian, you both have children or both do not have children, you both want children or you both don't want children.

Try to define what you are looking for without eliminating possible matches. When I become single, I make a list of "wants" and a list of "needs." It helps to narrow down the possible matches. Once you begin to meet a few potential partners, you'll know if, for example, education beyond high school is a want or a need. You could, and really should, revisit your list from time to time. As you change, your list should be adjusted accordingly. We certainly aren't the people today that we were ten years ago. If you know what you need, you can be better prepared when you do meet a guy. If he has what you want — let's say he has an amazing body—it might not matter that he doesn't keep a tidy apartment. You can just hang out at your place.

WANTS AND NEEDS

What if he has something you need—he's honest and likes to talk - but he doesn't exactly turn heads? Ultimately, you decide if your list is up-to-date ... maybe you need to review it again.

The flowers will still bloom, no matter how you feel.

CONTRIBUTIONS

Before I get too serious with a guy, I like to ask myself, "What can he contribute to my life?" I had a life before I met him, as did he. To merge two different lives/lifestyles calls for many discussions. It's a time to think realistically and be a little selfish. Bottom line ... what will he bring into the relationship to enhance your life?

At this point of a relationship, it's a good time to delve into some of these topics before you become too committed to him.

Sharing stories about past relationship experiences could be beneficial. Learning about what worked for each other and what did not - without getting into every sordid

27

detail - could provide each of you with information you may need to apply to your relationship together. For example, you would learn about how each other communicates. Does your initial discussion start out soft, subtle and serene? Does it remain pleasant and informative until the end or does it begin to feel like an interrogation?

Along with learning about communication styles and personal space, financial expectations and obligations are important topics to cover sooner rather than later in a relationship. The dynamics can be different depending on who has what and how much—not to mention what is considered shareable. Keep in mind, he may allude to having money, but this may not mean he will contribute to your vacations, wardrobe, rent/mortgage, etc. He could have undisclosed credit card debt, alimony or old student loans to pay. Just because he does all the "inviting," let's not assume he will always pick up the tab, especially in this modern age where women are earning their own money. Candid discussions regarding finances are crucial to a successful relationship lifeline.

CONTRIBUTIONS

Unless you were born into royalty, you are not a princess, so don't act like one. Do you think "princess" is on his list of wants and needs? Probably not, but it may end up on his pros/cons list! He may call you his "princess" as a sign of affection, which is sweet and endearing, but to demand materialistic items or catered-to activities will be short-lived.

Something to remember at this point in the relationship: When your lives are beginning to merge, be honest and open about what you want, need, and feel. If something doesn't feel in balance to you, you need to let him know you want help in certain areas. It's also important to remember that there will be times when he needs more from you as well.

In past relationships, there were times I felt I gave 100% and received 0% in return. In the beginning of my relationships, I tend to "spoil" my love by taking care of the groceries, then cooking dinner and cleaning up the mess, regardless of whose house we are at ... I also tend to plan the weekend get-aways, which most often leaves me holding the bill ... once our relationship starts to evolve, I start to drop subtle hints of requesting help – but sometimes it's too late. I have to remind myself that keeping score can be detrimental to a relationship.

An additional thing to consider at this point in the relationship is "internal" baggage, such as personality quirks or emotional traits. Consider the challenges posed by dating someone with social anxiety. Are you willing to date someone who is terribly uncomfortable at theme parks?

Internal baggage can include: insomnia, depression, or hypochondria. He, himself, may not realize these are topics that needs to be discussed; you'll just have to wade through it or bring it up casually. Ask your new potential partner, "How do you feel about going to theme parks, concerts, or waiting in grocery store lines?" I know that sounds silly, but how else are you going to get to know someone unless you ask questions? Most people love to talk about themselves, so throw a question his way and see what you can learn about him. Then see how that matches up with your wants and needs.

On the flip side, think to yourself, or even write down, what you can contribute to his life. Do you have unresolved issues, fears of regret, fears of settling, or fears of commitment? Do you have the time, space, and energy to give to your new relationship interest?

I once met a guy during a time when my personal calendar was full, but he was nice and fun to talk to so I tried to squeeze in time to get to know him. However, he wanted more of my time than I could offer. I was upfront and honest with him, expressing that I simply did not have the time or space in my life to contribute to a new person. His feelings were hurt because he felt there was chemistry between us and he wanted to begin a relationship with me, but I was unable to fill his expectations of seeing him on a regular basis.

Being honest with him lessened my guilt about moving on from him. I can only hope it cleared up the situation for him, versus not returning his calls or texts and causing him to wonder what he did wrong.

A pack of gum will lasts twice as long if you chew half a piece at a time.

EXPECTATIONS

Once I met a guy who instantly wanted me to be his girlfriend. I replied, "I just met you. I need some time, at least three months to get to know you … THEN I can decide if I want to be your official girlfriend." During the three-month holding pattern, he kept asking me to be his girlfriend.

Fed up with the topic, I finally asked him, "What is your definition of a girlfriend?" He replied, "Don't be intimate with anyone else."

What? That's it? THAT is what this has been all about? Noooo problem. I was interested in him and only him, so I agreed to be his girlfriend. I didn't feel the need for a title after only having known him a short time, but it was important to him for us to have a "label." It gave him a sense of security. I already felt secure with what I wanted to give and receive. The only expectation I had was to have a good time when I was with him.

However, it turned out his expectations were different than mine. Slowly, but surely, after spending several months together, his expectations of me began to surface. One example, and I am not kidding, was the expectation he had for my kitchen sink to be clear of dishes. *MY* sink? At *MY* house? *MY* dishes! It surprised me that this was so important to him. I mean, come on, there's a war going on and you care about DISHES? Despite my reservations, I tried to fulfill this expectation, but I found myself feeling bitter each time I stood in front of my sink washing the dishes before his arrival. His expectation of me agreeing to be his girlfriend was instant; his expectation of me having an empty sink came months into our relationship.

In my next relationship I made an effort to have an empty sink—not because my new interest expected me to do the dishes, but because I wanted to do them. Having learned what to do and what not to do from a previous relationship, I made an effort. They didn't always get done, but I no longer felt insecure about the few dishes that remained in my sink because I got them done most of the time. Not all relationships are the same, but you do learn from each of them. (I will repeat this statement throughout the book.)

Since no one (okay, only a small percentage of the population—I don't want to disregard the psychics of the world) can read your mind, it's a good idea to try to pull as much information from your new interest as possible. If you have expectations of him, find creative ways to communicate them.

It's not always easy to communicate because you don't want to hurt his feelings, or get your feelings hurt. But you certainly do not want to let little things build up inside your head and then have a release of negative emotions that could lead to an unnecessary argument. On paper it sounds easy enough to communicate, but the reality is that you don't know what each other is going through at work, or with family, or friends. So it's more often a delicate situation.

Single - YES! Lonely - NO!

One creative way to communicate your needs can be to make it into a game. Each of you begins a sentence with what you want or need at that point in the relationship. Maybe in the beginning you received a lot of affection, but as time moved on you felt he was less giving in that department. He may want more alone time or time with his friends. He will need to tell you that with an idea of how much time or what "alone time" means.

Be sure to listen when it's his turn to speak. You can show him that you are listening by looking him in the eyes and by not interrupting him.

You may need to play this game more often than you'd like because things change daily or weekly. What once was an issue may no longer suffice as a topic. If you think you've communicated your needs and they are still not being met, try again to express your concerns delicately—you do not want to enter into the nagging category.

There's a saying—choose your battles. Look at the big picture—whose quirk is it anyway? If he doesn't replace the toilet paper roll, you have to decide if changing it yourself is something you want to do because you are thankful enough that he at least sets a new roll out for you, or you could leave a cute sticky note out in the bathroom as a subtle reminder that may take care of that problem for you. It's creative, yet non-abrasive, and less threatening.

If you feel you can't or don't want to live up to his expectations, you can always hit the eject button. You, at this point, have no obligation to him.

Thoughtful thinking can keep you from sinking.

OBLIGATIONS

I think there are small things you are obligated to do for him, such as random acts of kindness, whether they get acknowledged or not. A few examples that have worked well for me in the past include (but are not limited to): having creamer in the house for his coffee, if he prefers that over milk. Stocking his favorite cocktail or, if he enjoys making breakfast, having some bread and eggs on hand for his visits. Voila! French toast!

The possibilities are endless. It's the small things you can do for your partner to keep him happy. Let him know you care about his happiness. Little things such as shaving your legs, having his favorite aromatic candle lit upon his arrival, or giving him control of the television can mean a lot to him, even if he isn't consciously aware that you're doing them.

Consider in-the-bedroom treats like sexy pajamas or soft music before bedtime. These types of small tokens can be reciprocated with having the oil changed in your car or projects done around the house. After a cozy night with you, he'll probably whistle while he works!

This is a two-way street. If he is not returning random acts of kindness, and you feel you've shown examples of how well these small efforts are a large part of your happiness, ask him to take out the trash as he's leaving. It's not exactly random, but it will work, and maybe next time he'll do it without being asked.

Relationships are like speed bumps: Slow down and proceed with caution.

UNDER CONSTRUCTION

After having met someone and deciding that he is someone you'd like to spend some quality time with, the next step is building the relationship—think like a builder to create a strong foundation. This doesn't happen overnight, so don't try to rush it. Construction takes time—great construction takes a lot of time and effort.

The beginning of a new relationship is often referred to as the "Honeymoon Stage." So let's build the "stage." Once you've decided that this guy is worth the extra time and energy, you'll need the proper tools to start building.

Tool #1: Communication. It may seem overwhelming at first when you realize how much about this new guy is unknown to you. Take your time and look for opportunities to ask questions that go deeper than "What's your favorite football team?" You may ask about his dreams, his goals, his current focus in life.

Taking a walk together will present the opportunity to talk openly; you can start with comments about the scenery, and let the moments meld into deeper conversations. Here's a moment you can determine if you are walking close enough to him so you can grab his hand or link your arm with his. This may be the time to bring up the topic of affection. How comfortable is he with public displays of affection? Are you compatible when it comes to initiating the moves? Are you on the same page? Are you even reading the same book? (Metaphorically speaking, of course.)

Tool #2: Trust. There are more ways to trust him in a relationship than the obvious "don't cheat on me" kind of trust.

Do you trust his driving? You are precious cargo, after all. Do you trust that when you take him to meet your friends and family that he won't drink too much and make a fool of himself? Do you trust that he is where he said he would be? If he needs a babysitter, tuck him in quietly, softly close the door of this relationship, and move on.

During the construction period of your relationship, you can decide if he is a fixer-upper or if he has solid foundation to build upon.

Your "stage" should have balance. Not too much weight on the "I see you too much" side and not too much on the "I don't see you enough side."

If you decide to recycle this man, try to release him without excessive issues to deal with, like anger, for just disappearing. Try to keep the Mother Earth dating pool as clean as possible by being honest with him ... as I did in a previous chapter when I knew I didn't have the time or space to contribute to a new relationship.

Catch some fireflies in a jar ... open it up – they will go far.

HOW CAN I MISS YOU IF YOU DON'T GO AWAY?

Have you ever given a dog a new toy? He tends to look at it for a while, sniff it, walk around it, then maybe bat it with his paws a bit. He is getting use to it. He's deciding if it's something he should be wary of or something playful.

When the dog decides he likes the toy, he may begin to carry it around with him, possibly take it to sleep with him at night, and begin to feel its comfort. But after a while, it may become old news, and you might see him tossing it aside or overlooking it. But if you take the toy away, he may begin look for it because he would miss it, and he would want it back. Give the toy back to him after several days and he will love it again, like new. This is much like a new relationship. If you see your new interest day after day after day, there's no time to miss him. Sure, it's great in the beginning. You truly want to be with this guy; you can hardly get your fill of him. However, after some time, it's hard to miss him because he is always there.

Is it nice to have someone in your life who wants to be with you all the time?

Yes.

Is it nice to be missed?

Yes.

Is it okay to miss someone you care for?

Yes.

But ... how can I miss you if you don't go away?

One of my past partners asked me to call him multiple times a day even though we saw each other often. He would request a phone call when I woke up in the morning. I wondered, "Why"? I haven't done anything earth-shattering since I spoke to you before going to bed. I SLEPT! But it was his request that I call, so I did. It was solely out of obligation to fulfill his request.

46

HOW CAN I MISS YOU IF YOU DON'T GO AWAY?

To me, beginning each day with a call to just say "Good morning" seems routine. I also don't think it's necessary to call daily on my lunch hour. What I had for lunch that day was food. Yes, I ate food for lunch. If it happened to be a great meal, or if I visited a new restaurant, I'd share that information.

Thank goodness for text messaging. "Thinking of you" can suffice for days when I have nothing pertinent to discuss with a guy. If I do have something pertinent to tell him or vice-versa, then a phone call is best. For example, if I have a horrible day at work and need to blow off some steam, I know talking to him will help to calm me down just by hearing his voice. Or if I decide to go out of town with a girlfriend for the weekend, I'll call to let him know that I won't be around. If I win the lottery—he'll be getting a phone call!

In order not to drown, stay on higher ground.

SMOOTH AS WAVES

The heart of the relationship is the time things start to get real. In the beginning, I tend to avoid him if I have a head cold because I don't want to scare him away with all the tissues lying around on the floor by the couch or the noises associated with a cold. But after investing quality time with him, I begin to let my guard down; I feel secure that he isn't going to run away if I blow my nose really loudly. I feel that we are floating right along in our new relationship. The "honeymoon stage" has been constructed. There's communication. There's trust. I think it's smooth sailing from here. I mean, what could go wrong, right? The heart of a relationship should be like an artichoke heart ... the best part.

However, lurking in the water are some obstacles which can be encountered: sandbanks, hidden rocks, driftwood. And let's not forget about the ever-changing tides. High tides, low tides.

In this section, topics discussed in earlier conversations may surface. Let's be honest, once the Honeymoon Stage settles, as all foundations do, you or your partner may not be as considerate as you were in the initial stages of the relationship. Are each of you still on board with helping around the house? Random acts of kindness? These types of things may start to diminish as the relationship gains longevity. Sparks of affection may become dormant like seaweed lying on the shore.

My point is that none of my relationships have been completely smooth sailing. Life changes, situations arise, feelings get hurt. These types of things happen in every relationship. How do you weather the storms?

There will be obstacles that come along, but if there's a strong foundation, and you are attempting to meet each other's expectations, then you have to rely on good 'ole fashion communication.

Waves are not smooth, but waters do calm down. At times there is comfort and then there are times you could feel stuck in the current and have to stay afloat.

As I've experienced, this is the time in relationships when the tide can change. Things about each of us that were easily tolerated, overlooked, or even embraced as charming in the beginning may become long-term issues due to the quality and quantity of time we've invested. The constant silly one-liner jokes or the repetition of stories about previous relationships ... they may have been endearing in the beginning, but as time goes on it's like a crack in the hull.

While I might have a good idea of how to react based on my past relationships, I don't really know what to expect from him—yet. As I've learned, not all relationships are the same, but from past experiences, I can steer towards what to do and away from what not to do.

Have you dated a lone surfer? I have. They're used to being independent and dealing with situations on their own;

they can retreat when they sense an issue arising in order to wrap their heads around it. In the case of a guy like this, it's hard work to get him to communicate. When I feel it's time for him to ride his wave safely to the shore, I'm ready to let go and I find myself in search of a better wave.

Have you ever dated a lifeguard type? I have. Lifeguards are attentive to problems as they begin to surface and generally can get a perspective on how to deal with the situation. But lifeguards often see themselves as heroes who "save" others from danger. If he's sitting high on a tower assessing the situation, he may not be interested in my perspective.

Once I dated a guy who thought I had the potential to fall overboard, so he smothered me like an oversize life jacket. I felt like I couldn't catch my breath. I found myself swimming away from our "ship." I needed some time and space for myself.

I try to settle on the idea of dating someone as if in a two-person kayak. We can go through the motions together. When my arms get tired, my partner can be counted on to take over and get us both to safety. There'll be times when

SMOOTH AS WAVES

I'm paddling to the right and he is paddling to the left, but communication will get us straightened out, and help us to avoid capsizing and get going in the same direction again.

Two beds are better than one hot head.

THE DUPLEX COMPLEX

I love LOVE … falling in love and being in love is a wonderful experience. Finding someone to share your life with is a beautiful thing. You may decide to see and be with this person day in and day out. Sounds great!

Once I found love with a neighbor. I lived in an apartment complex for most of my young adult life; I had a wonderful group of neighbor friends that would relax by the pool and share life stories. One day a very handsome guy moved in right next door to me – how lucky was I?! We started dating and it was wonderful; we shared everything and even joked about cutting a secret door in the wall of our adjoining apartments so we wouldn't have to go in and out of our front doors. All the neighborhood friends knew we started dating and were supportive and welcomed him right into our circle. That all sounds wonderful, right? A year or so after dating him, I realized that I no longer wanted to be in this relationship because of his unruly children. His parenting skills did not live up to my expectations, so the relationship ended … but we still lived next door to each other and, to say the least, it became a bit uncomfortable to see him on a daily basis. The neighboring friends became more like therapists for each of us – the dynamic of our circle changed. So from my past experience, I would not recommend dating a neighbor.

Society has laid some unwritten ground rules— stepping stones for the progression of a long lasting relationship: you meet, you date, you love, you move in together (whether married or not). Since I prefer the untraditional route, I choose to build a strong, loving, stable foundation and when I'm ready to take the next step, I would prefer to move close in proximity to one another. This way, no one has to purge and merge …

Introducing … The Duplex Complex.

I have an internal complex about sharing a permanent space with the loves of my life. I don't want to pack, unpack and possibly have to someday pack and unpack again; been there – done that. A long-time boyfriend of mine sold me on the idea that if he and I moved in together, it would save me money, and at that time in my life that sounded reasonable. Once we moved in together, the dynamic of our relationship changed and within a year, I was gathering boxes and looking for a place to live on my own. I need to feel settled and secure in my space.

A compromise I've dreamed of is to move close to each other. This way we'd have our own space, I'd get to keep my treasures *AND* we'd get the compassion and love when either of us want or need it.

I've worked hard for my possessions, both big and small, and I'd like to keep hold of the treasures I've acquired over the years; they signify my wants and needs. When I have a yard sale, I rarely put items in the sale that hold personal value to me. In the duplex theory, I can keep my soft bed and matching dressers. I would get to keep my couch and decorative rugs. My over-priced Tupperware and Pampered Chef items would stay in the condition I want: no scratches on the Teflon, no warped lids that no longer fit the container. My side of the house would continue to reflect my style. I would have to do my own dishes—but when I wanted to. My toiletries could be spread out over the bathroom counter without having to make space for anything else. There'd be no need for my love to pack an overnight bag—he lives next door!

He, too, would be able to keep his treasures, decorate in his own style, and do his own dishes!

We could share responsibilities of having a pet, watering the lawn, and checking the mail.

Spending time with my family on my side of the house? I could invite him over. Spending time with his family on his side of the house? I could make a casserole to take over.

Sad or mad? Sleep alone in MY bed. Love, lust, or just want to snuggle? Sleep together.

Positive emotions take slow motions.

EMOTION MOTION – OVERRULED!

We all experience emotions. Here are my top four: Happy, Sad, Silly, Mad. It's how we handle our emotions that makes up a large part of who we are. One emotion that can be a challenge to handle is jealousy.

My definition of jealousy: A combination of doubt, insecurities, hurt, and confusion all mixed together.

In my early thirties, I traveled quite a bit for work, which took me out-of-town on a monthly basis – there were boyfriends who would constantly call me to see where I was, who I was with and what I was doing. This was frustrating to me because most of the time I was working! Yes, there were dinners and functions I would attend with customers, but again ... I was working! It was their jealousy of the unknown.

Since I'd been working on keeping a healthy relationship, I would try to communicate my feelings—my guy should respect how I felt. I obviously cared about him or I wouldn't have taken the time to share my thoughts.

Some of my past loves spent too much time at the office; some have had a hobby that takes time away from our relationship. These types of situations promote a void which left me with too much time to myself. I think of all the stay-at-home mothers or teachers with summers off from work; they may feel that their love is not available when they want/need him to be.

Self-discipline and emotional control needs to be practiced when the green-eyed-monster rears its ugly head.

I just take a few deep breaths, and calm myself before I fill up with anger or resentment. The more intimacy deepens in a relationship, the more internal struggles can ensue. Internal emotional struggle is actually an indication that feelings are deepening. These concerns could morph into jealousy if I am feeling insecure.

62

EMOTION MOTION – OVERRULED!

Sometimes I have to decipher my feelings, I ask myself, "Is it actually jealousy that I am experiencing or do I feel disrespected? Disheartened? Disappointed, or disenchanted? Does the situation justify my emotions?"

Please don't allow *your* insecurities to be the repeat offender in your break-ups.

Separate ways equate to a temporary daze.

BREAK-UPS

How can you become single again if you don't go through a break-up?

Break-ups are difficult, emotionally draining, yet, if you've become unhappy in your relationship, they become necessary to be able to move on with your life.

If you thought your relationship was going to progress into a real life fairytale, and the relationship ends—it sucks.

If it were more casual, it may not be as heartbreaking, but it can still bring you down once the relationship is over.

It may take a few days or weeks, but at some point you may begin to dissect the situation and realize the time you've invested in this one person. Many times you can see it coming. Sometimes you are blind-sided. If/when you can tell the relationship has run its course, do you prefer to be the dump-er or be the dump-ee? You may say to yourself, "This is just not working out the way I thought it would." In this case, you need to share those thoughts with your partner. If you decide to end the relationship after discussing your feelings, then you'd be the dump-er. If your partner decides to end the relationship, well, then you're the dump-ee.

It's no fun ending a significant relationship. It can trigger feelings of abandonment and maybe bring up bad memories from past break-ups. The feelings you're experiencing are valid. Try to learn from what has happened so you can use this knowledge in your future relationships.

A few examples of my past break-up have included, but are not limited to:

1. The Classic: "It's not you; it's me" which includes not fulfilling relationship expectations. My partner or I are not living up to each other's wants and/or needs.

66

2. The Long-Distance Relationship: Moving out of town creates inconvenience. I've started a few long-distance relationships, but eventually the novelty wore off.

3. The Too Much Baggage/Drama: I began to realize that I didn't want to raise his children after having spent a few days, weeks, months, or years with them. I realized that his ex-files are a little more complicated than I originally thought.

4. Passive-Aggressive Sabotage: I have sensed him distancing himself – I began to subconsciously sabotage the relationship before the break-up even happened. For instance, I've played the dump-ee role a few times before and haven't fully healed from the emotional damage, my viewpoint might have been distorted. I might see things that aren't there and begin to act in ways that actually push my love away.

Some people end a relationship before they give it a chance, especially if they sense change coming from their partner. Once again, communication is important. You might be thinking he is upset with you when really he has something totally unrelated on his mind. This goes both ways. You might be sending out signals that something is wrong, and if you don't communicate, you may create distance between you and your partner. That distance might be the thing that tears you apart.

I tend to linger in unhealthy relationships because I can not find the "exit." Whether I feel I will not be able to find the passion and intimacy in my next relationship, or feel I don't want to make the effort to start a new one.

Avoidance of the inevitable will only set you back. Time will pass whether you leave the relationship or not.

After unsuccessfully trying to work through the glitches, the healthiest thing for both you and your partner is to break up in a respectful way. You both deserve to be happy. Sometimes the most loving thing you can do is to let go.

Once I dated a guy who proposed a question (noooo ... not *THE* question!). He asked me, "Are we good TO each other or are we good FOR each other?" I took quite some time, three weeks to be exact, to ask myself that same question. Turns out we were good TO each other, but not

FOR each other. Hence, I became single again. It was a fair and mature break-up—one for the books. Today he is one of my closest friends. We are still very good to each other, and I believe our friendship survives because we were open in our communication about how the relationship was going.

Whether the break-up is mutual or not, the act of breaking up is generally followed by the grieving process: denial, anger, bargaining, depression, and acceptance. Grieving isn't just for death; it's for any type of loss, and a break-up is definitely a loss. You may feel like you are carrying a heavy burden which prevents you from eating regularly; you may think chips and salsa make a well-balanced dinner–it's okay temporarily, but nutrition is important so you can remain healthy and maintain a clear mind. Try not to over-indulge with food–you'll want to look and feel good when you're ready to meet someone new. Keep in mind break-ups happen every day all around the world. You may feel alone, but you are not alone. Grasp the concept that this guy will no longer hold a special position in your life; perhaps his role in your life will change into something other than boyfriend. But it's also possible that he will fade out of your life completely. Be ready to accept either of these changes.

Some suggestions to move you to acceptance:

If you feel the need to get rid of everything that reminds you of him, go ahead. You may feel like tearing up all the photographs of the two of you, but don't do this too soon; you never know if he will resurface in your life and then you've destroyed your tangible past.

If you think you'd like to go to therapy, go ahead.

If you feel like going shopping, give yourself a budget that you are comfortable with, and go ahead.

Maybe take a new exercise class or start a new book. Stay busy, relax your mind, and enjoy being single again.

Your friends are there for you. Many of my long-term friends live in different areas. I am not able to sit with them at a coffee shop to vent my feelings about my break-up, but

BREAK-UPS

I know they are a phone call away; they are 'hear' for me.

Nesting time is investing time.

MOVING FORWARD BY GOING
BACKWARDS

I'm guilty of breaking up and getting back together, a cycle that is unhealthy for both parties. Sometimes I've felt that getting back out there in the dating world starts to feel like a job interview. I get tired of being asked all the recycled questions when getting to know someone new.

If that starts to happen to you, you may feel like calling up an ex to fill in the gap. You think it's safe because you already know him, his quirks, his habits, his outlook on things and, most importantly, you know the reasons it didn't work out in the first place. An old boyfriend can be

73

as comfortable as your weekend sweatpants, but you know you can't wear those pants every day.

"Reunion Guy" vs. "Rebound Guy."

"Reunion Guy" is someone you reunite with. He could be someone you dated in your past and happened to run into at a local venue. Maybe you re-united through social media, or he's someone from high school who just moved back to town or someone you used to work with whom you had a secret crush on – he is "Reunion Guy." "Reunion Guy" becomes a close "friend." You may or may not have special romantic feelings for "Reunion Guy," but he is someone you feel comfortable with and it's nice to spend time with a familiar face, for now.

"Rebound Guy" is the guy you meet when you feel you need someone to fill in the gap between long-term partners. "Reunion Guy" can become "Rebound Guy" as you may just need someone to hang out with while you're preparing to get yourself back out there in the dating world.

MOVING FORWARD BY GOING BACKWARDS

Be sure there is clear communication of what each of you is looking for in that time of your life—the crossroads. It's nice to have someone of the opposite sex to check in with every now and then, maybe go for coffee or see a movie; as long as either of these guys don't become too attached, then hanging out with them should be okay. Try looking at it as a part-time job; skip the interview process and move into scheduled meetings. My place or yours?

This may be awkward if/when you or he finds a new mate. So this chapter is a rough suggestion, as all relationships differ.

Please do not re-connect with a past love if you know the outcome would be detrimental. If you know he is looking for marriage and that is not something you are looking for with him, unless you communicate and there's an agreement, this could lead to hurt feelings. It would be a significant break-up all over again. However, if you feel there are unresolved issues and there may be a better outcome this time around, then try dating again.

Here are some guidelines for "friends with benefits":

Do make him feel comfortable at your home, but don't let him nest there. Friends with benefits don't get to do their laundry at your place.

Do make plans with him, but nothing too serious. If you plan a casual happy hour, you can offer to pay half the bill. Don't let him wine and dine; it can give false hope.

Do establish boundaries. Maybe he is not the only one you're dating, but you've both agreed not to climb in bed with anyone else. Don't lead him on emotionally.

Do have long discussions about your day. Don't excessively discuss the fun times you enjoy with other friends. If you receive a phone call, keep it a short conversation; give him the attention he deserves while you're spending quantity time with him.

Do respect him and the time you are both sharing with one another. Don't show interest in anyone else while in your friend's presence. Don't be sneaky about it either!

Much like a caterpillar turns into a butterfly ... we too can transform.

TRANSFORMATION

Having never been married, and therefore never divorced, I will comment on this through a short story. It's called:

Tawanda Panties

A lady friend of mine, twenty years my senior, was going through a divorce. It was a rough patch in her life; she was neither the initiator nor the guilty party. We talked often over the phone and we visited when we could. We have traveled together over the years and each have a special place in the other's heart.

After many long phone conversations with her, I began to understand the difficulty she was experiencing when she had to face her soon-to-be ex-husband in court–the proceedings; it seemed overwhelming for her. Imagining what my friend was going through, I felt as though I should do something to give her a smile and a laugh.

Because we have traveled with each other, I knew her wardrobe style. Sure, I could have gotten her a scarf or a purse or sent her new earrings, but what I was really searching for was not a tangible item–it was something more powerful.

Knowing her wardrobe style, I knew her preference of "unders." Her comfort zone was wearing what we referenced as "big girl panties." I decided my gift to her would be a matching bra and thong set. There. That was it. She would smile. She would laugh.

She actually wore them! She wore them to her court appearances. We called them her TAWANDA PANTIES! They gave her strength and courage. They gave her confidence. They were symbolic!

I shared the story of the "unders" with a close relative of mine who also went through a divorce. She understood how powerful something that seemed insignificant could be. Her profession encouraged her to wear flat, comfortable, sensible shoes. But on those court days when she had to face her soon-to-be ex-husband, she wore high heels. Just a change in her shoe type gave her the confidence she needed.

My girlfriend no longer wears thongs and my relative no longer wears high heels, but when they needed a little boost of power, they found it.

Unlike divorce, death of a partner is something that, unfortunately, I have experienced. It was a tragedy for all. The unthinkable that I have not stopped thinking of for many, many years. Suicide. One day I had a boyfriend and the next day I was single again.

This is a different type of break-up altogether. Typically, when you end a relationship, there is just cause. You or your partner no longer want to be together. With the death of a loved one, however, you are typically still in love— with no plans (at that time) to part ways. It hurts on a much deeper level. Breaking up seems insignificant compared to losing your loved one. Forever.

Single - YES! Lonely - NO!

This is not the time for you to stop living; it is, however, the time of your life for grieving. There is no time limit to how long you will grieve. You will continue to wake up in the morning. You should brush your teeth, but hey, maybe there'll be days you never leave home, and then this is up to you. You should try to eat sensibly, but sometimes Ritz crackers will suffice. Be sad, be very sad, but know your friends and family will be there for you – they'll check up on you and want the "ole' girl" back again.

You'll have a new routine—one which will not include hearing or seeing your loved one. You'll not hear that special ring tone you set on your phone just for him. You'll lie down at night and miss the comfort of him next to you, but the sun will still rise the next day. Try to make your day better than the previous one.

Just know there'll be a time when you have to deal with things you feel uncomfortable with—if you lived together, you will have to deal with the financial aspects. But someday you will feel comfortable tossing out the old razors or putting his personal belongings in a consolidated space. No need to start throwing everything out–just

TRANSFORMATION

consolidate ... you may want that special blanket of his to wrap yourself in while watching your favorite movie.

A head held high is one thing that never has to come down.

LET'S LIGHTEN UP!

I'll start this section with a joke. Please remember, this is just a joke:

What is the difference between a boyfriend and a husband?   45 minutes.

What is the difference between a girlfriend and a wife? 45 pounds.

(Insert laugh here)

Speaking of "extra" pounds that you may be carrying around, don't get yourself upset about it. If you become uncomfortable with how you feel or look, you will do something about it.

When you're ready, I hope that you choose a healthy way to trim down. Be concerned about your health, not the number of pounds shown on the bathroom scale. The bathroom scale has one job; its job is to tell you how much you weigh. It will not tell you how pretty, sweet, funny or thoughtful you are. Keep that in mind.

I once dated an "over-achiever" when it came down to a healthy lifestyle. Although his intention for me to follow in his footsteps was genuine, it left me feeling inadequate. When he and I took a walk, I felt as though he were taking me OUT for a walk. I wanted it to be two people who cared for each other, holding hands, talking about our day—not who got to the next intersection first.

Although I enjoy cooking, I don't qualify as a world-renown chef. While dating this Jack LaLanne character, we took turns cooking meals for each other. I got the impression he thought his cooking was superior to mine. This made me feel like it was a contest: my-dinner-is-better-than-yours type thing.

LET'S LIGHTEN UP!

In a past relationship of mine, my boyfriend and I DID have cook-offs, which were fun and something we did together in the kitchen.

"Who made the better burger?"

"Here, taste mine."

"I like this ingredient you used."

"Let's do this again."

I have two points here. First, if there's an area of your life that's important to you, then it's important to share it with your partner. For me being active and healthy is important, but I don't want it to be forced it upon me. My passion was to spend quality time with these guys, in and out of the kitchen.

Second, it's important that you go into a relationship feeling good about who you are and keep that healthy self-image in check. So if you start letting the guy you're with make you feel less beautiful and special than you know you are, step back and figure out why. It may be time to check out.

You can live vicariously through others, or you can live.

WING-WOMAN

The term Wingman is an actual reference to an Air Force flight pattern. It's not a "man" per se; it's the aircraft which flies behind and to the right of the lead aircraft.

In today's society, the term Wingman has taken on the same meaning, but a different style. It still means "I got your back," but it is describing an actual human.

Here's an example: A group of guys go into a bar. One of the guys sees a gal he wants to dance with or talk to, so the friend, the wingman, goes over to the lady or group of ladies and strikes up a conversation. He breaks the ice, and before you know it, the girl or group of ladies is comfortable enough to join the guy or group of guys. Often times, guys, especially shy guys, need a little help in the "meeting the ladies" department. The wingman is there for protection, and support.

An introduction: She is your partner-in-crime, she is your shoulder to lean on, she is your confidante. She is your Wing-Woman!

Here's a homework assignment. Ask one of your closest gal-pals to assist you. She can be single or married; it doesn't matter in this scenario. Map out several grocery stores or hardware stores in your area. Set aside a few hours one day to peruse the "market." Take a recipe, a cookbook, or a list of items needed for home improvements. You don't even have to purchase anything on this trip. But be on the lookout for single guys who can answer a few questions for you. What single guy wouldn't want to share his knowledge and insights about tools, construction work, or the best paint to use with a couple of ladies? Stroking a guy's ego is generally a good way to get his attention. Pay attention to what he has to say—it gives you time to measure your interest level in him. Maybe he's not the one you want to hang out with, but with your wing-woman by your side, you have an easy out if he turns out to be a tool. (hardware store humor)

If you choose to go to a grocery store, where do the men hang out? The meat department. It would be funny if it were called THE MEET DEPARTMENT. Ask questions of the butcher—innocent enough. You can inquire about the difference between grilling and barbecuing. Even if the butcher is not your type, he is there to help. Then you might feel comfortable asking male shoppers what they think of your recipe. The task is to get conversations going and mingle with people. They might just open up, and you could get a little party started right there in the aisle.

Farmers markets are another fun place to hang out. Choose a fruit or vegetable you know nothing about and begin your inquiries. You and your friends will enjoy this experience, just laughing and being light-hearted. No need to give your number out; be the gatherer. Plant a few seeds because sometimes "fruit" looks good on the outside, but once you take a bite or start to cut it up, it's internally bruised. This ties back to our previous section covering "internal baggage" and learning from past relationships. If you think you've made a connection with someone, why not invite him to meet you for coffee or a cocktail? Take your wing-woman with you until you feel safe enough to venture off with this guy on your own. No expectations, no obligations. Don't start planning a wedding or anything yet. Just have a fun time!

Keep in mind, you may not be single for long, so while you are, take advantage of it.

Afterword

Relationships of all kinds enhance your life. Some relationships last throughout your life; others are short-lived. No matter the length, every relationship adds something to your life.

Just remember to treat yourself with respect and expect others to treat you that way too. If you expect trust and honesty from your partners, you must earn it.

Relationships are fun! Enjoy those that come your way ... whether you end up sharing the rest of your life with someone or you travel from single to single again.

Will You Kiss Me If I Snore?

Walking away from the years you kissed me when I snored

In my subconscious mind, I wander and I find ... that in my

heart and conscious mind, I was really bored.

Of your silence and routine ways ... I look forward to a

bright future and exciting days.

~ C. Lee Miller, written after a significant break-up

GLOSSARY

Speed Dating

An organized group of singles mingle in person during a specific time frame

Singles sit across a table from the opposite sex and talk, usually for a few minutes

When the time frame is over, they move to the next table and talk with someone new, and so on and so on ... hoping they find chemistry with someone to exchange phone numbers.

Some events charge a fee, others are free

Sport Dating

Not organized

Playing the "field" by getting and giving phone numbers

Dating multiple people casually, informally

Trying to score a home run

Single – YES! Lonely – NO!

On-line Dating

Signing up on a computer dating service; some charge a fee upfront, others do not

Looking through pictures, reading blurbs of others' interests

Finding someone to connect with for more private conversation

Could lead to a date or a friendship

"Traditional" Relationship

Meet someone special

Share interests and activities

Grow together

Love unconditionally

Make and execute plans to unite

There is no end - 'til death do you part

"Untraditional" Relationship

Meet someone special

Share interests and activities

GLOSSARY

Set conditions - as time permits

No set plans to unite

There's an end - when it's no longer fun or convenient

Intimate/Romantic Relationship

Meet someone special

Share interests and activities

Build trust - begin to love

Go to bed at night and wake up together in the morning

Repeat

Platonic Friendship

Meet someone special

Share interests and activities

Do not become intimate

Stay in touch

"Friends" with Benefits

Set guidelines

Go to bed at night and wake up together in the morning

Don't get too comfortable - there's usually an end

Single – YES! Lonely – NO!

Significant Break-up

Meet someone very special

You both have strong emotional feelings towards one another

You each share all you have to give in the relationship

You feel a real connection

You begin to make plans to share your lives

You want to be with no other … ever … until one of you decides to break your bond and most importantly—your heart.

About the Author

C. Lee Miller, bachelorette, lives in Southern California.

She has never married and feels qualified to inspire others.

She volunteers when she can, which includes taking care of her neighbors' pets while they are out of town.

She enjoys spending time with friends and family, near and far.

To share comments, questions or concerns …

C. Lee Miller can be reached through her website:

www.c-lee-miller-author.com

For poems, inspirational stories, and a train of blogs, please visit:

www.fromsingletosingleagain.com

Wants And Needs

DATE:

WANTS   NEEDS

_____   _____

_____   _____

_____   _____

_____   _____

_____   _____

_____   _____

_____   _____

_____   _____

_____   _____

_____   _____

www.ingramcontent.com/pod-product-compliance
Lightning Source LLC
Chambersburg PA
CBHW060116050426
42448CB00010B/1893